AF799800

Published by AVA Credit Inc.
Toronto, Ontario, Canada
avacredit.ca

ISBN: 978-1-0696203-1-6

First Edition — March 2026

Contents

About This Book

The term "AI" has become so bloated and abstract that many professionals have lost sight of what they are actually dealing with. They hear "AI" and think robots, job replacement, science fiction, existential threat. Or the greatest invention in human history and a civilization-level shift. Some expect to plug it in like a lamp and have it do their job for them. Others refuse to touch it altogether. The concept has no edges. It floats somewhere between hype and fear, between magic and mystery, untethered from anything concrete.

This book is not about any of that. It is not about AI as a civilization-level phenomenon. It is not about artificial general intelligence or an autonomous future where machines think like humans. It is about you, sitting at your desk, talking to a language model, getting work done. One human, one tool, working together. That is the foundation everything in this book builds from.

This book is built on a single conviction: the human-AI partnership is the most powerful use of this technology. From that foundation, it answers one question: what does a professional need to understand to work effectively with AI? The answer is not technical. It is a mental model.

Early AI guidance focused on tools, features, and use cases. It cataloged what AI can do without explaining how to think about it. The result is experimentation without direction. Professionals try AI, get inconsistent results, and conclude it does not work for them. This book takes a different approach. It establishes a first principles architecture for human-AI collaboration: five chapters, one mental model that holds regardless of which tools you use or how the technology evolves.

First principles thinking is a way of reasoning that distills complexity into core definitions. You identify what is irreducibly true, strip away assumption and analogy, and build your understanding from there. The architecture in this book was built the same way: not by cataloging what AI tools do, but by asking what is fundamentally true about how humans and AI work together.

That process produced five chapters and one mental model.

The appendices provide optional depth for readers who want to understand the mechanics beneath the framework. This includes how the technology works, the building blocks of AI, and data scope and responsibility. They are not required to work effectively with AI. The five chapters are complete on their own.

This book is not a collection of tips. It is not a catalog of features. It is a single coherent system designed to be learned once and applied indefinitely. The architecture is minimal and complete. The sequence is deliberate. The outcome is earned.

This book is written for the professional who seeks a reliable way to use AI to achieve speed and precision within their field of expertise, and who is ready to Work with AI.

The Mental Model

Working effectively with AI is built on five elements. Each answers one fundamental question. Together they produce a predictable outcome. This is the complete mental model.

THE FOUNDATION-FIRST SEQUENCE

WHO → **WHAT** → **DO** → **HOW** → **WHY**

1	2	3	4	5
Ground Zero	**The Interface**	**The Playbook**	**The Skill**	**The Outcome**
WHO: THE UNIT	WHAT: NATURAL LANGUAGE	DO: RGI FRAMEWORK	HOW: PROMPTING	WHY: SPEED + PRECISION
Captain and Copilot. You are accountable. AI is ready.	Tell machines what you want in plain language and be understood.	Retrieve, Generate, Interact. Every use case maps to one of three.	Goal, Context, Format, Reference, Refine. Communication is the craft.	Earned, not promised. What emerges when the mental model executes correctly.

The sequence matters. Role definition makes sense of the interface. The interface enables the playbook, which is what you can do with AI. The playbook requires communication skill. The skill produces the outcome. Skip any element and everything downstream becomes guesswork.

Introduction

You have heard the promises. Ten times productivity. Radical efficiency. Competitive advantage through artificial intelligence. Maybe you attended a keynote address or watched a demonstration. Maybe you sat through a company training session. You left interested. Then you returned to your desk, opened an AI tool, typed a few prompts, got inconsistent results, and moved on with your day.

You are not alone in this experience. Many people who try artificial intelligence follow the same pattern: initial curiosity, a handful of experiments, inconsistent results, then abandonment. Not because the technology failed. Because nobody gave them the mental model needed to operate it reliably.

That is the gap this book closes. The answer is not tips, hacks, or prompt templates. It is a first principles architecture: a structured sequence that builds the mental model needed to make AI work reliably.

First principles reasoning works differently from learning by observation. Instead of imitating what seems to work for others, you distill complexity into its core definitions and build up from there. Instead of asking what worked before, you ask what is fundamentally true now. Instead of applying familiar patterns to unfamiliar technology, you identify the irreducible elements.

Applied to artificial intelligence, this method produces something specific: a mental model built on what does not change. Tools will change. Interfaces will evolve. Capabilities will expand. But the fundamental relationship between human expertise and machine capability, the way you communicate with it, the actions you can perform, and the outcome that emerges when you execute correctly will remain true. Your competitive edge is not the AI. Everyone will have the AI. Your competitive edge is your skill collaborating with it.

FIVE CHAPTERS. ONE MENTAL MODEL.

Chapter 1 · WHO is involved, and what role does each party play?

Chapter 2 · WHAT is the interface between human and machine?

Chapter 3 · What tasks can you **DO** with this technology?

Chapter 4 · HOW do you communicate to get reliable results?

Chapter 5 · WHY — The outcome of executing the mental model.

By the end of this book, you will have the mental model that makes AI predictable and immediately useful.

We begin with the most fundamental question: who are you working with?

CHAPTER 1 · WHO

Ground Zero

Before methodology, before prompting. Role comes first.

Every collaboration begins with role definition. Before you learn techniques, before you write a single prompt, before you explore what artificial intelligence can do, you need to answer the most fundamental question: who is involved in this work, and what role does each party play?

The answer is simple. You are the captain. Your AI is the copilot. This is not a metaphor. It is the precise definition of an operational relationship that determines everything that follows.

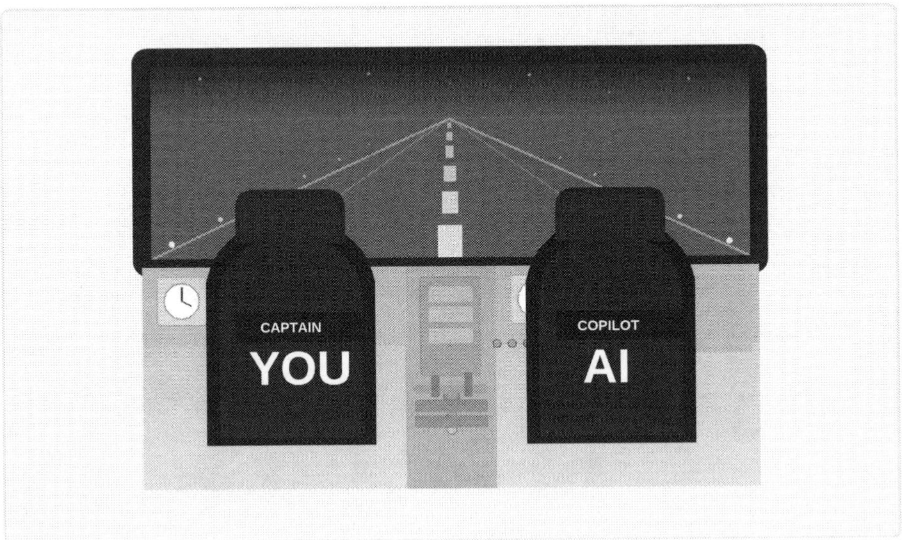

The Captain

EXPERTISE · JUDGMENT · INTENT

You set the destination and make the calls. You bring the context, the experience, and the domain knowledge that no machine possesses. You are accountable for the outcome.

The Copilot

SPEED · SCALE · PRECISION · MEMORY

A language model that processes and generates digital content. It works without fatigue, follows instructions precisely, and executes in seconds what would take you hours. Always ready. Waiting for your instructions.

As captain, you make decisions. You bear responsibility for outcomes. You exercise judgment shaped by years of education and experience. You understand the things no machine can fully grasp: the dynamics of your organization, the preferences of specific clients, the constraints of particular situations, the nuances that separate technically correct from practically useful.

Your copilot handles execution. It processes information faster than any human could. It maintains perfect recall. It generates drafts, analyzes data, retrieves relevant information, identifies patterns, and produces outputs at a speed that simply was not available to you before. But it does not decide. It does not judge. It does not take accountability. It cannot replace your judgment because it does not have judgment. It has capability.

This distinction defines how the relationship works. You do not ask your AI what to do. You tell it what you need and evaluate what it produces. You do not defer to its suggestions. You assess them against your expertise and make decisions. You do not trust its output blindly. You review, refine, and verify. The captain decides. The copilot executes.

The captain and copilot model prevents two common failures. The first is over-reliance: expecting AI to make decisions it cannot reliably deliver. People who fall into this trap ask their AI to solve problems that require judgment, get generic responses, and conclude the technology does not work. They are right that it does not work as a captain. It was never designed to be one. The second failure is under-utilization: treating AI as a novelty rather than a tool. People in this category never move beyond simple queries. They use their AI like a search engine, never discovering that it can draft, analyze, build, and iterate alongside them through sustained collaboration.

The captain and copilot relationship avoids both extremes. You maintain accountability and judgment while gaining execution capability that did not exist before modern AI and language models. You keep what only humans provide: context, expertise, decision-making authority. You access what machines excel at: speed, scale, tireless execution, perfect recall.

This relationship is irreducible. You cannot skip it. You cannot reverse it. Once you understand your role and the AI's role, everything downstream makes sense: what to expect, what to provide, how to evaluate, and why something fails when it does. Without this clarity, every interaction becomes an experiment. Some experiments succeed. Many do not.

You + AI. Captain + Copilot. The unit.

One human, one tool, working together. Everything else builds from here.

I know my role. I am the captain.

What Is Generative AI?

The natural language interface. The revolution is that you can talk to a computer and be understood.

The most important shift introduced by generative AI is not speed, scale, or automation. It is the interface. For the first time in the history of computing, professionals can communicate with machines using plain human language and be understood. No programming. No commands. No technical mediation. You describe what you need in your own words, and the system figures out how to deliver it.

> *Generative AI lets humans use natural language to communicate with computing systems to retrieve, generate, and interact with the knowledge, content, and decisions needed to get work done.*

It connects everything. The unit from Chapter 1 communicates through natural language. The three capabilities you will learn in Chapter 3, retrieve, generate, and interact, are what that communication unlocks. The interface is the bridge between the human who knows what needs to happen and the machine that can help make it happen.

What Made This Possible

In June 2017, a team of researchers at Google published a paper titled "Attention Is All You Need." It introduced the Transformer architecture, a new way for machines to process language. Before the Transformer, computers could follow instructions, execute code, and automate repetitive tasks. But they could not understand you. They could not read a paragraph and grasp what it meant. They could not take your request, stated in your own words, and figure out what you actually needed.

The Transformer changed that. It gave machines the ability to pay attention to the relationships between words, to understand context, to process language the way humans naturally use it. Every conversation you have had with an AI assistant. Every document you have asked it to summarize. Every email it has helped you draft. Every file retrieved from your own systems. Every report generated from your own data. Every decision informed by your own workflows. All of it traces back to that paper and the architecture it introduced.

The Inversion

For decades, human-computer interaction meant learning the computer's language. You learned commands, code, syntax, specific procedures. The machine did not adapt to you. You adapted to it. This created a permanent barrier: only people willing to invest significant time learning technical skills could leverage computational power.

Generative AI reverses that relationship entirely. The machine now adapts to you. The interface is no longer buttons and menus. It is conversation. You describe what you need in your own words, and the system responds in kind. This is not a convenient feature. It is the structural change that makes artificial intelligence accessible to every professional, regardless of technical background.

BEFORE

Human learns the machine's language. Code, commands, syntax. Access gated by technical skill.

→

AFTER

Machine learns the human's language. Plain words, natural conversation. Access gated by clarity of thought.

What This Means for You

Consider what this means if you have spent years developing domain expertise. You know how to analyze situations, advise clients, navigate complexity, and make sound decisions. That expertise is not obsolete. It is more valuable than ever, because now you can direct computational power with the same precision you bring to your craft. The skills you already have, communication, explanation, evaluation, transfer directly.

This creates a fundamentally different learning curve. With conventional software, you memorize where features are located and what buttons do what. Your capability is limited by how much of the interface you have mastered. With natural language, your capability is limited only by how clearly you can describe what you want. The limiting factor is no longer technical skill. It is clarity of thought. You do not need to become technical. You need to become deliberate.

THE INTERFACE

Analyze this quarter's performance data attached and identify the three most important trends. Present as an executive summary for the board.

If you can explain what you need to a colleague, you can explain it to your AI.

The Essential Insight

There is one thing that must be understood about how this works. The system does not know what you are thinking. It only knows what you provided. When you send a message, the model reads your input and generates a response based on patterns learned from vast amounts of text. Vague input produces vague output. Specific, well-structured input produces precise, useful responses. Your job is to bridge the gap between your intent and your expression, to translate what you mean into language the model can work with.

The simplicity of the natural language interface often leads to a misunderstanding. Because your AI responds fluently, it is tempting to assume it understands context, intent, or consequences the way a human does. It does not. Fluency is not understanding. A language model processes input and generates output based on patterns and probabilities. The interface makes the interaction feel intuitive, but intuition should not be confused with judgment. This is why the natural language interface must be understood in the context of the unit established in Ground Zero. The human brings intent, expertise, and accountability. The AI provides speed, recall, and linguistic fluency. Natural language is the bridge between the two.

Access, Not Intelligence

The natural language interface determines access. Any domain that relies on language, knowledge, reasoning, or decision support can be augmented through conversation. Every knowledge domain runs on language. Contracts are language. Analysis is language. Advice is language. Decisions are language.

This is why generative AI appears everywhere at once. It is not because AI has suddenly become many different tools. It is because the interface is universal.

I know the interface. It is conversation.

CHAPTER 3 · DO

What Can You DO with AI?

Three actions. Every meaningful use case maps to one of them.

Once you understand the unit and the natural language interface, the next question is practical: what can I actually do with this? The answer is simpler than most people expect. Despite the explosion of tools, features, and use cases, there are only three fundamental actions you can perform with generative AI. Every meaningful application reduces to one or more of these actions. Together, they form the playbook for working with AI.

Retrieve. Generate. Interact. This is the RGI Framework. It is not a categorization of tools. It is a taxonomy of work. It describes how professionals already operate, now compressed and accelerated through a conversational interface. You already retrieve information, generate content, and interact with colleagues to calibrate decisions. RGI does not invent new behavior. It names the behavior you already perform and shows you that your AI can now participate in all three.

R	G	I
Retrieve	**Generate**	**Interact**
ASK · FIND · SEARCH	WRITE · IDEATE · CREATE	INSTRUCT · QUERY · COLLABORATE · ACT
Use AI as a knowledge engine. Surface what already exists in a form you can use.	Use AI as a production engine. Create new content based on your direction.	Use AI as a thinking partner. Refine, question, iterate, and shape outcomes together.

Retrieve: Ask | Find | Search

Retrieve is the act of using AI as a knowledge engine. It replaces manual searching, scanning, and synthesis with direct extraction through language. You are not asking the AI to create something new.

You are asking it to surface what already exists in a form you can use. "Pull the key terms related to liability and termination from this contract and summarize them in plain language." That is retrieval. The AI ingests your request, locates the relevant information, and presents it. What previously required you to read forty pages now takes seconds.

Generate: Write | Ideate | Create

Generate is the act of using AI as a production engine. This is how you draft emails, reports, analyses, proposals, presentations, images, audio, video, and code. Anything that needs to be produced from a prompt. Generation accelerates the mechanical work of expression. It does not replace thinking. It clears the path so thinking can move faster. "Based on the meeting notes attached, draft a client-ready executive summary with three recommended next steps. Format as a PDF and an email-ready HTML version." That is generation. Raw material in. Two polished deliverables out. You review, refine, and send.

Interact: Instruct | Query | Collaborate | Act

Interact is the act of using AI as a thinking partner. This is where AI shifts from a static tool to a dynamic collaborator. Interaction involves dialogue, refinement, questioning, and iteration. You challenge assumptions. You explore alternatives. You guide the system through multi-step reasoning. "Walk me through the risks of this proposal. Now argue the other side. What am I missing? What questions should I be asking that I have not asked?" That is interaction. You are not getting an answer. You are shaping one. At its most advanced, Interact includes Act: directing your AI to take independent action within your systems and workflows, not just respond to prompts.

How They Combine

These three actions are distinct, but they often combine in a single workflow. You might retrieve information from a document, generate a draft based on that information, and then interact with your AI to refine tone, structure, or logic. Consider preparing a presentation: retrieve recent performance data, generate an outline based on key metrics, interact to refine the narrative, retrieve industry benchmarks for comparison, generate draft slides, interact to sharpen the language. One workflow, all three capabilities, completed in minutes.

The Boundary

The power of RGI lies in its completeness. There is no fourth category for professional work. Researchers who study AI usage broadly do identify a fourth behavior called Express, covering personal expression, emotional processing, and social conversation. It is real, but it falls outside productive professional collaboration. Any work-related expression, communicating ideas, articulating positions, conveying feedback, is already captured within Interact. If a task does not fit Retrieve, Generate, or Interact, it is not a professional AI task. This clarity is what makes the playbook durable.

> **Three actions. Every task has a home.**
>
> Retrieve what exists. Generate what is needed. Interact to refine the result.

The RGI Framework works because it describes what AI actually does, not what any particular tool offers. Retrieve, Generate, Interact. Those are the operations. They apply whether you are drafting an email, retrieving documents, or orchestrating an enterprise workflow. When you know what AI does at its core, you know what to ask for. You stop guessing and start directing. And when something does not work, you know which operation to revisit. That clarity holds at every level of professional use.

Without this framework, users face cognitive overload. AI seems to do everything and nothing simultaneously. Usage becomes random. Prompts are improvised. Results feel inconsistent. Confidence erodes. With RGI, experimentation becomes intentional. Results become repeatable. You stop wondering what AI can do and start seeing how any task breaks down into these three operations.

I know what I can do. Retrieve. Generate. Interact.

CHAPTER 4 · HOW

How to Communicate with AI

Prompting is how you talk to AI. Master prompting, master AI.

You understand your role. You understand the interface. You understand the three fundamental capabilities. Now comes the skill that determines whether you get excellent results or mediocre ones: how you communicate what you want.

This is prompting. Prompting is communicating with your AI. That is all it is. It is not a technical trick or a stylistic flourish. It is the act of communicating your intent clearly enough that your AI can deliver what you are actually looking for. The same AI, given different prompts, will produce dramatically different results. This is not a flaw in the technology. It is a reflection of how closely output quality is tied to input quality. Here is the fundamental insight: AI capability is essentially unlimited, but AI knowledge of your specific situation is essentially zero. The gap between capability and knowledge is bridged entirely by the quality of your communication.

Prompting is a professional skill. Same AI, different prompts, different results.

THE PROMPT FORMULA

Goal + **Context** + **Format** + **Reference** + **Refine** = **Precision**

Effective prompting has five elements. You do not need all five in every interaction, but understanding each one gives you control over output quality.

Goal means stating clearly what you want. Not what you are generally interested in, but what specific output you need. "Write a report on our top clients" is vague. "Write a two-page performance report for our Q3 client accounts, highlighting gaps and recommended actions" is a goal. The more precisely you state what you want, the more precisely your AI can deliver it.

Context means providing the information your AI needs to deliver relevant output. Who is the audience? What do they already know? What constraints apply? The AI cannot read your mind. It cannot see your screen. It does not know your clients, your organization, or your preferences. Everything it needs to know, you must provide. This is the single biggest determinant of quality.

Format means specifying how you want the output structured. A summary, a comparison table, a narrative memo, a set of options. The same information in the wrong format is useless. Specify format upfront and you get output you can actually use.

Reference means pointing your AI toward examples, standards, or source material that illustrate what good looks like. "Use the same structure as last quarter's report but for the current data." "Match the tone of this document but make it accessible to a non-technical audience." References show rather than tell, and are often faster and more accurate than lengthy description.

Refine means iterating on output until you get what you need. The first result is a starting point. Review it. Identify what works and what does not. Give specific feedback. The AI does not get offended by criticism. It does not care how many revisions you request. It is designed for iteration. Most people treat AI output as binary: it works or it does not. The best operators treat every response as a draft they can shape.

VAGUE PROMPT		COMPLETE PROMPT
"Write a report on our top clients." Goal only. No context, no format, no reference. Generic output guaranteed.	→	*"Write a two-page status report on our top ten client accounts. The audience is our leadership team. They want to see where we are on target, where we are at risk, and what actions are recommended for each. Use the same structure as last quarter's review. Lead with the exceptions."* Goal + Context + Format + Reference. Immediately useful output.

The Judgment Principle

There is one insight that separates skilled operators from casual users. Prompting is not about extracting answers. It is about applying professional judgment through language. The better the judgment, the better the prompt. A senior professional with deep domain expertise will get better results than a novice, not because they know more about AI, but because they know more about the problem. Their prompts carry sharper intent, richer context, and clearer standards. AI does not elevate weak thinking. It amplifies whatever thinking is present.

Power Prompting

Once the formula is internalized, more sophisticated techniques become available. **Think-first prompting** asks the model to walk through its reasoning before giving a final answer, which reduces errors and reveals assumptions. **Role prompting** assigns a specific perspective to steer tone and depth: "Respond as a senior advisor reviewing this report before it goes to the client. Flag anything that is unclear, overstated, or missing." **Sequential prompting** breaks complex tasks into ordered steps delivered as separate prompts, improving accuracy at each stage. And there is a technique that functions as a secret weapon: you can ask your AI how to prompt it, and it will tell you. These are awareness items for now. The skill develops through practice.

Common Pitfalls

The patterns that consistently produce poor results are predictable. Vague prompts with no specific outcome force the AI to guess. Overloaded prompts that combine multiple goals create confusion. Leaving format unspecified means the system chooses structure arbitrarily. Accepting weak output without iterating leaves value on the table. And missing context, failing to explain who, what, why, and for whom, causes accuracy to drop because the AI lacks the information it needs to respond precisely. Every one of these pitfalls is a communication failure, not a technology failure. And because they are communication failures, they are fixable using skills you already have.

Users and Operators

The most important shift occurs when you stop treating AI as a question-answering machine and start treating it as a collaborator. Two professionals with access to the same AI and the same information can produce completely different results. One gets generic, unreliable output. The other gets clear, useful, trustworthy work product. The difference is not intelligence. It is communication. That is what separates casual users from operators.

I know how to communicate.

CHAPTER 5 · WHY

The Speed–Precision Principle

This is what the mental model is for. Speed and precision are the outcome.

When the captain and copilot relationship is clear, the natural language interface is leveraged fully, the three fundamental capabilities are directed with precision, and communication is effective, something specific emerges. Not productivity improvement in the abstract. Something concrete: you move faster without sacrificing accuracy. You collapse the time a task requires while increasing the precision and quality of the output. Both at once. That is the Speed–Precision Principle.

Speed without precision is recklessness. You move quickly but create problems that take longer to fix than the time you saved. Precision without speed is irrelevant in competitive environments. You get things perfect while others get things done. Before AI, professionals chose between these two constraints constantly. Respond quickly with generic information, or respond slowly with personalized detail. Review a document at the surface level in an hour, or conduct a thorough analysis over a full day. Draft something fast and revise it later, or build it carefully from scratch. The trade-off was permanent. It defined the rhythm of knowledge work.

That trade-off is gone.

BEFORE

Choose speed or precision. Fast work is shallow. Thorough work is slow. The trade-off defines the rhythm of professional life.

→

AFTER

Speed and precision operate together. Friction disappears. Cycle time collapses. Output quality increases. The trade-off dissolves.

When a professional executes the mental model correctly, friction disappears from the work itself. Research no longer stalls momentum. Drafting no longer delays decision-making. Formatting no longer interrupts flow. The repetitive, mechanical elements of knowledge work stop acting as bottlenecks. The distance between intent and execution collapses. You move from idea to output, from question to clarity, from hypothesis to draft, without unnecessary delay. The AI handles execution. You handle expertise. This is the proper division of labor between human and machine.

The result is that iteration becomes the real superpower. Each pass sharpens the result. Each cycle lands closer to the target. Errors surface earlier. Feedback is immediate and the output is better.

The Self-Reinforcing Cycle

When you experience speed and precision operating together for the first time, something changes. You do not need convincing about the value of AI. You just experienced it. And you start looking for other applications. Faster feedback leads to better judgment. Better judgment leads to higher-quality decisions. Higher-quality decisions reinforce trust. Trust drives deeper adoption. The cycle compounds. This is why adoption happens quickly when the mental model is right. Users do not need inspiration or motivation. They need to experience the outcome once.

What Becomes Feasible

The Speed–Precision Principle changes what is feasible in your work. Tasks you previously could not tackle because they would take too long become possible. Analysis you did not do because it was not worth the time becomes routine. Communication you abbreviated because drafting took too long becomes thorough. Quality improvements you knew would be better but could not justify the time investment become standard. Your work shifts upward. Instead of spending time on execution, you spend time on judgment. Instead of drafting, you are editing. Instead of researching, you are synthesizing. Instead of creating from scratch, you are directing.

This is true across every domain. Try it, see what works, fix what doesn't, and move to the next version. The professional who can think something and execute it with both speed and precision can now fail fast, learn immediately, and arrive at a better result.

The Mental Model, Not the Technology

This outcome does not emerge from raw AI capability alone. Many organizations have access to the same AI models. They do not all achieve speed with precision. The difference is the mental model. When professionals understand their role, they maintain appropriate oversight. When they understand the interface, they communicate clearly. When they understand the playbook, they know what to request. When they master communication, they get reliable results. These elements working together produce the outcome. Remove any element and it degrades. This is why the mental model matters. It is not just cleaner thinking. It is the path to the result.

Speed and precision. Not promised. Earned.

The outcome of executing the mental model correctly. Once experienced, unmistakable.

I know why it matters. Speed and precision, earned.

CLOSING

Be Curious

You now have a clear mental model for how human-AI collaboration actually works regardless of which tools you use, which industry you work in, or how the technology evolves.

The unit: you are the captain, AI is your copilot. The interface: natural language, the most fundamental breakthrough. The playbook: Retrieve, Generate, Interact, three actions that give every task a home. The skill: prompting is communicating with your AI, and communication quality determines output quality. The outcome: speed and precision, earned through execution.

Each element depends on the ones before it. Role definition makes sense of the interface. The interface enables the playbook. The playbook requires the skill. The skill produces the outcome. Skip any element and everything downstream becomes guesswork.

THE FOUNDATION-FIRST SEQUENCE

WHO → WHAT → DO → HOW → WHY

What is happening right now is not a trend. Generative AI is a structural shift in knowledge work on the scale of the printing press, electricity, and the internet. Each of those breakthroughs changed what was possible, not incrementally but permanently.

What will change is the surface area. Interfaces will become more seamless. AI will appear in more systems, more workflows, and more moments of your work. The distance between intent and execution will continue to shrink.

What will not change is where responsibility lives. Judgment will remain human. Context will remain human. Accountability will remain human. The AI will continue to assist, accelerate, and amplify, but it will not decide what matters. As capabilities grow, the importance of clear roles increases, not decreases. It makes judgment more consequential.

This is why the mental model endures. It is not tied to a version, a platform, or a moment in time. The real power is not the AI. It is what becomes possible when you work with AI as a collaborative partnership.

Curiosity is the driving force. It breaks through hesitation. It is the operating principle at every stage of this work. It is what gets you to open the tool for the first time. It is what pushes you past the plateau when basic use becomes comfortable. It is what drives you to bring a novel problem to your copilot when there is no template and no precedent, and to think it through together until something new emerges. This is not a beginner's posture. The professional who has been working with AI for years still needs it, because the problems get harder, the stakes get higher, and the most valuable work happens at the edge of what is known.

You are the captain. Natural language is your interface.
Retrieve, Generate, and Interact are your playbook.
Clear communication is your skill.
Speed and precision are your outcome.

Be Curious.

Appendix A

AI Building Blocks

THE TAXONOMY

AI → ML → Deep Learning → GenAI → LLMs

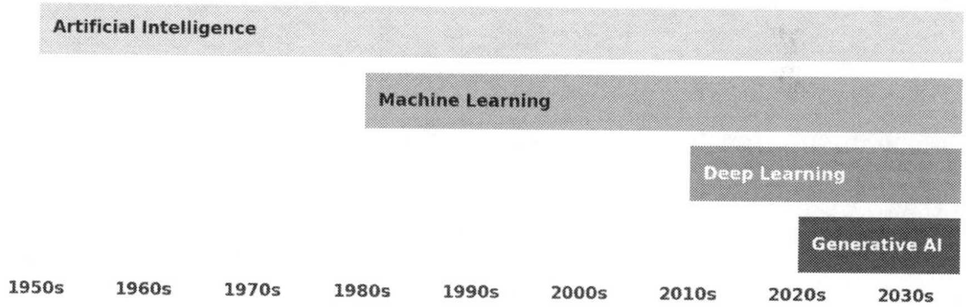

Artificial Intelligence

Any system that pursues a goal by processing data in a way that mimics human judgment, without step-by-step human rules. AI swaps hard-coded "if-this-then-that" logic for software that adapts.

Algorithm

Step-by-step instructions or rules a computer follows to solve problems or perform tasks.

Machine Learning

Branch of AI focused on building systems that learn from data rather than relying on explicit programming, making software more accurate and responsive over time.

Deep Learning

Powerful subset of machine learning that uses layered artificial neural networks to identify complex patterns in large, high-dimensional datasets. As neural networks grow in depth and scale, so does their capacity to interpret complex information.

Generative AI
AI systems designed to create new, original content such as text, images, audio, or code by learning patterns from existing data and then generating context-appropriate outputs on demand, rather than merely analyzing or labeling data.

Large Language Models
Foundation Models trained chiefly on text and optimised to read and write human language. Using the transformer's self-attention mechanism, they predict one token at a time across billions of parameters, yielding fluid prose, sharp summaries, multilingual translation, and conversational Q&A from a single prompt. In practice, an LLM is the engine behind most chat interfaces, writing assistants and enterprise systems in use today.

Foundation Models

Large-scale neural networks that power today's generative AI landscape. Their emergence began with the 2017 introduction of the transformer architecture, detailed in the landmark paper "Attention Is All You Need," which redefined how machines process language. The landscape has evolved rapidly from text-only models to sophisticated multimodal systems capable of processing and generating content across text, images, audio, video, code, and even specialized domains like protein structures and robotic control. Their scale, flexibility, and transferability make them the critical layer beneath the generative AI ecosystem, allowing professionals to collaborate with intelligence at speed and scale.

What Made Generative AI Possible?

Three breakthroughs converged. First, the invention of the Transformer architecture in 2017, which radically improved how machines understand and generate language by enabling models to capture context more effectively. Second, an explosion of digital content, from websites and e-books to source code and corporate filings, created the vast training data needed to teach these systems how to write, reason, and respond. Third, advances in computing power, especially the rise of specialized chips like GPUs and TPUs, made it feasible to train and deploy large-scale models at speed and scale.

The Generative-AI Tech Stack

Generative AI is not a single tool. It is a layered stack. At the base are hardware and cloud systems: GPUs, TPUs, data centers, and high-speed networks. Above that are GenAI platforms, including LLMs, vector databases, orchestration tools, and secure APIs that read, reason, and generate across data types. At the top is the human-AI adoption layer, where skills, workflows, governance, and culture shape real-world impact. This layer enables three modes of interaction: Augmentation (today's co-pilot), Agency (emerging assistants that act on our behalf), and Automation (fully autonomous execution).

The Professional Services Stack

Professional services work is built on judgment, trust, and regulation, three areas where a human in the loop is non-negotiable. In relationship-driven, compliance-sensitive fields like finance, law, consulting, accounting, and healthcare, the near-term opportunity lies in the Augmentation layer: an AI co-pilot handles the heavy lifting while you apply judgment, ensure compliance, and manage client nuance. Real enterprise value comes not from models alone, but from how professionals adopt and apply them.

The field was born in the summer of 1956, when a small group of researchers gathered at Dartmouth College with a bold hypothesis: that every aspect of learning and intelligence could, in principle, be described precisely enough for a machine to simulate it. The decades that followed produced bursts of progress and periods of disillusionment that researchers came to call "AI winters." Early programs could solve logic puzzles but broke down in the real world. Expert systems encoded human knowledge into rules but were brittle and could not learn. The cycle repeated: promise, limitation, retreat.

What changed the trajectory was machine learning. Instead of programming rules by hand, researchers built systems that learned patterns directly from data. In 2012, a deep learning model dramatically outperformed traditional approaches in image recognition, proving that neural networks could achieve results hand-engineered systems never would. In March 2016, a deep learning system called AlphaGo defeated Lee Sedol, one of the greatest Go players in history, in a match broadcast live to millions. In Game 2, AlphaGo played Move 37, a stone placement that contradicted centuries of accumulated wisdom and turned out to be the decisive play. AI moved from academic research into public consciousness.

The decisive moment came one year later. In 2017, a team of researchers published "Attention Is All You Need," introducing the Transformer architecture. Previous language models processed words sequentially, limiting their ability to understand context across long passages. The Transformer processed entire sequences simultaneously, allowing models to grasp relationships between words regardless of distance. This single breakthrough made it possible to build the large language models that power the generative AI systems in use today. The journey from Dartmouth to the Transformer took six decades. The journey from the Transformer to the tools on your screen took less than six years.

Professionals are not expected to code or train large language models, but a basic understanding of how they work is now part of modern professional literacy. Knowing what happens under the hood helps you judge when an LLM is the right tool, craft precise prompts that deliver relevant output, and explain results clearly to clients, colleagues, or stakeholders. In short, this is mechanics for operators, not a deep dive for engineers.

An algorithm is a set of step-by-step instructions a computer follows to solve a problem or perform a task. In generative AI, algorithms train large language models by guiding them to detect patterns in data, adjust internal settings, and learn how to generate useful responses. If the model is the engine, the algorithm is the blueprint and tuning process used to build and optimize that engine. Professionals do not need to know how to write algorithms, but understanding that they exist helps demystify how these systems work and why they are so powerful.

Every Large Language Model follows the same three-stage cycle:

STAGE 1	→	STAGE 2	→	STAGE 3
Training		**Tokenization**		**Inference**

During training, the model reads billions of tokens drawn from books, filings, websites, code, and more. By repeatedly guessing the next token and comparing its guess to the correct answer, it learns the statistical rhythms of language, a method called self-supervised learning. A second pass, often guided by human feedback, fine-tunes the model so its answers line up better with real-world intentions. Training is where the model acquires its broad knowledge.

When you type a prompt, the model moves to tokenization. Your text is chopped into sub-word units called tokens, and the model processes them inside a fixed context window. That window defines how much information the system can "see" at one time and therefore shapes cost, speed, and output length. A 50-page contract or report may need to be chunked or augmented with retrieval tools because its token count can exceed the window.

Finally, the model enters inference. It calculates the most likely next token, appends it, recalculates, and continues, literally word by word, until it decides to stop. Settings such as temperature and top-k sampling govern how creative or conservative this process feels: low temperature for drafting precise language, higher for brainstorming and ideation. Different decoding strategies explain why the same model can produce a tight executive summary in one moment and a free-flowing thought piece the next.

Understanding these three stages turns a large language model from a black box into a usable, predictable tool. Each part of the RGI Framework connects directly: **Retrieve** tasks are limited by the context window, **Generate** tasks respond to decoding settings, and **Interact** tasks depend on how clearly you prompt and refine.

THE GENERATIVE AI STACK

Generative AI is a layered stack. At the base is hardware. In the middle are platforms. At the top is where professionals operate — in three modes that represent a trajectory from today to where the technology is heading.

AUTONOMOUS

Automation

AI executes end-to-end from human-set instructions.

DELEGATED

Agency

AI acts independently on your behalf across people and systems.

COLLABORATIVE

Augmentation

Humans and AI work together as thinking partners. This is where you operate.

LAYER 3

Human-AI Adoption

Skills, workflows, and governance that enable safe, effective use of GenAI tools.

LAYER 2

Generative AI Platforms

LLMs, vector databases, APIs, and tools that read, draft, and reason across data types.

LAYER 1

AI Infrastructure

Physical and cloud systems: GPUs, TPUs, power grids, networks, and data centers.

Understanding the stack, the stages, and the modes turns generative AI from a black box into a tool you can operate with intention. The professional who understands where they sit in this architecture does not just use AI. They direct it.

Appendix B

Data Scope

THE DISTINCTION

Many conversations about AI draw a sharp distinction between "public AI" and "enterprise AI." The distinction is often misunderstood. It suggests that there are different kinds of intelligence at work, or that enterprise systems are fundamentally more advanced. That is not the case.

The difference is not intelligence. The difference is data scope.

Data scope defines what information an AI system is allowed to access, retrieve, and reason over. Every interaction with AI operates within some data scope, whether the user is aware of it or not. Understanding this boundary removes confusion, reduces misplaced fear, and clarifies professional responsibility.

The interface does not change. The playbook does not change. The skill does not change. Only the information boundary changes.

OPEN DATA SCOPE

General world knowledge

The AI operates using public information and broad reasoning capabilities. This is the default environment for most widely available AI tools.

Well suited for learning, experimentation, drafting generic content, brainstorming, explaining unfamiliar concepts, and creating reusable templates. This is where most professionals begin and where skill is developed.

Does not include internal documents, client information, proprietary workflows, institutional policies, or confidential records. The AI is not omitting this information. It is not allowed to see it.

→

BOUNDED DATA SCOPE

Organization-specific knowledge

The AI operates with access to a defined body of internal knowledge: training materials, policies, procedures, curated documentation, or other organization-specific content. The scope is deliberately constrained. The goal is not breadth, but relevance.

Outputs become more consistent with institutional reality. Responses align with internal standards. Hallucinations decrease because the system is grounded in authoritative material. The behavior feels more reliable, not because the AI is smarter, but because it is better informed.

RESPONSIBILITY

Enterprise AI is not a more advanced version of public AI. It is the same interface, the same Retrieve-Generate-Interact playbook, and the same prompting discipline. What changes is the responsibility that accompanies access to information.

As data scope narrows, responsibility increases. When working with public information, outputs are exploratory and mistakes are low-stakes. When working with bounded data, outputs influence decisions, communications, and outcomes that matter. Errors can propagate. Trust becomes central.

> **The AI does not assume that responsibility. The human operator does.**

GOVERNANCE AND SHADOW AI

Governance is often framed as a limitation on capability. In practice it is a stability mechanism. It reflects the reality that context matters, errors compound, and accountability cannot be delegated. Once professionals understand how AI systems actually work, including their reliance on context and retrieval, governance stops feeling bureaucratic and begins to feel inevitable.

The most significant risk in professional AI adoption is not malicious misuse. It is casual use without boundaries: uploading client files into public models, mixing sensitive information into general prompts, trusting outputs without validation. This is shadow AI. In most cases it is not intentional. It is the result of an unclear mental model about where the boundary sits.

Understanding data scope prevents this. Enterprise AI is a platform that can produce the evidence the regulator requires, used within the workflows it was designed to govern.

Before using AI in any professional context, one question must be answered clearly: what information is this system allowed to see? If that answer is uncertain, responsibility is unclear. That is the moment to stop — not because AI is dangerous, but because professional accountability requires clarity.

CLOSING

> Working with AI is not about access to intelligence. It is about disciplined access to information. Professionals who understand data scope work faster, make fewer errors, and build trust over time. They do not need more tools or more complexity. They need clarity about boundaries and responsibility.
>
> The interface remains simple. The playbook remains universal. The skill remains human.
>
> Only the boundary changes.
>
> **And understanding that boundary is the difference between using AI and truly working with AI.**

Quick Reference Guide

Work with AI

THE UNIT

You are the captain. AI is your copilot.

You set the direction, apply judgment, and own the outcome. AI accelerates the work. You stay in control.

THE INTERFACE

Generative AI lets humans use natural language to communicate with computing systems to retrieve, generate, and interact with the knowledge, content, and decisions needed to get work done.

THE RGI FRAMEWORK

R

Retrieve

ASK · FIND · SEARCH

Use AI as a knowledge engine. Surface what already exists in a form you can use.

G

Generate

WRITE · IDEATE · CREATE

Use AI as a production engine. Create new content based on your direction.

I

Interact

INSTRUCT · QUERY · COLLABORATE

Use AI as a thinking partner. Refine, question, iterate, and shape outcomes together.

THE PROMPT FORMULA

Goal + **Context** + **Format** + **Reference** + **Refine** = **Precision**

THE OUTCOME

AI does not replace your domain expertise. It removes the lag between what you know and what you can produce, so you move faster without sacrificing accuracy. Speed and precision, both at once. That is why you Work with AI.

You are the captain. Natural language is your interface.
Retrieve, Generate, and Interact are your playbook.
Clear communication is your skill.
Speed with precision is your outcome.

Be curious.

About the Author

Matthew Dobson

Founder and CEO, AVA Credit Inc.

In October 2017, a University of Toronto AI/ML PhD student shared Google's "Attention Is All You Need" paper, the foundational architecture behind generative AI. Most people in financial services had never heard of it. Matthew Dobson read it and saw the future of professional work. Within two months, he filed the AI Credit® trademark in December 2017, one of the earliest registered applications of AI to financial services in North America.

What followed was not theory. After more than two decades in commercial lending, including senior sales and credit roles at GE Capital and TD Bank, he served as Chief Credit Officer for an institutional lending operation, where he built and deployed AI tools to assist underwriting across hundreds of live commercial finance transactions. These were real decisions, real capital, and real accountability. The conclusions from years of operationalizing AI in a live lending environment were consistent: AI's greatest value was not automation. It was augmentation. The professionals who treated AI as a collaborative partner outperformed those who treated it as either a replacement for thinking or a tool too risky to trust. That operational experience became the foundation for everything in this book.

In 2023, he founded AVA — Accelerated Virtual Analyst — a firm built from its origins around human-AI collaboration in financial services and enterprise AI enablement, later incorporated as AVA Credit Inc. in Toronto.

In 2025, he was selected for the inaugural Perplexity AI Business Fellowship, an invitation-only program bringing together executives and CEOs from Perplexity AI, NVIDIA, and the leadership of some of the most consequential technology companies, financial institutions, and venture firms in the world. That same year, he developed the RGI Framework for the practical adoption of AI in professional work and launched a national AI training initiative for Dominion Lending Centres Inc. (TSX: DLCG), Canada's leading mortgage network. Thousands of licensed professionals completed the program. The response was near-universal: the framework made AI predictable, practical, and immediately useful.

This book is the result. Every chapter traces back to a real deployment, a real training session, or a real conversation with someone trying to make AI work in their professional life. It is written for the professional who seeks a reliable way to use AI to achieve speed and precision within their field of expertise, and who is ready to Work with AI.

Matthew Dobson is the founder of AVA Credit Inc., a Toronto-based AI and financial services advisory firm. He is a licensed mortgage professional in Ontario, a dual citizen of Canada and the United States, and holds a B.Sc. from Western University. · avacredit.ca

IMPORTANT DISCLAIMER

This guide is intended for general informational purposes only. It provides a broad overview of considerations related to the use of generative AI in professional settings, including financial services. It is not tailored to the specific circumstances of any individual, firm, or jurisdiction and does not constitute legal, regulatory, or other professional advice. Readers should not rely on this guide as a substitute for personalized legal or compliance advice. Before implementing any generative AI tools or practices in your business, you are strongly encouraged to seek independent legal and regulatory advice relevant to your specific situation.

Work with AI

Foundation

The Mental Model for Professional AI

Made in the USA
Monee, IL
04 November 2026

67377007R00024